BARRIER-
BREAKER
BIOS

CLAUDETTE COLVIN

Civil Rights Activist

Cathleen Small

Cavendish
Square

New York

Published in 2020 by Cavendish Square Publishing, LLC
243 5th Avenue, Suite 136, New York, NY 10016

Copyright © 2020 by Cavendish Square Publishing, LLC

First Edition

Website: cavendishsq.com

This publication represents the opinions and views of the author based on his or her personal
experience, knowledge, and research. The information in this book serves as a general guide
only. The author and publisher have used their best efforts in preparing this book and disclaim
liability rising directly or indirectly from the use and application of this book.

All websites were available and accurate when this book was sent to press.

Library of Congress Cataloging-in-Publication Data

Names: Small, Cathleen, author.
Title: Claudette Colvin : civil rights activist / Cathleen Small.
Description: New York : Cavendish Square, 2020. | Series: Barrier-breaker bios |
Audience: Grades: 1-4. | Includes bibliographical references and index.
Identifiers: LCCN 2019009287 (print) | LCCN 2019015453 (ebook) | ISBN 9781502649591 (ebook) |
ISBN 9781502649584 (library bound) | ISBN 9781502649560 (pbk.) | ISBN 9781502649577 (6 pack)
Subjects: LCSH: Colvin, Claudette, 1939---Juvenile literature. | African American teenage girls--Alabama--
Montgomery--Biography--Juvenile literature. | African American civil rights workers--Alabama--Montgomery-
-Biography--Juvenile literature. | African Americans--Segregation--Alabama--Montgomery--History--
Juvenile literature. | Segregation in transportation--Alabama--Montgomery--History--Juvenile literature.
Classification: LCC F334.M753 (ebook) | LCC F334.M753 C6557 2020 (print) |
DDC 323.092 [B] --dc23
LC record available at https://lccn.loc.gov/2019009287

Editor: Alexis David
Copy Editor: Nathan Heidelberger
Associate Art Director: Alan Sliwinski
Designer: Christina Shults
Production Coordinator: Karol Szymczuk
Photo Research: J8 Media

Printed in the United States of America

TABLE OF CONTENTS

CHAPTER 1
Who Is Claudette Colvin? 5

CHAPTER 2
Sitting Up Straight 13

CHAPTER 3
A More Equal Society 21

Timeline 28

Glossary 29

Find Out More 30

Index 31

About the Author 32

This is Claudette Colvin as a young girl.

Colvin's school was named after Booker T. Washington.

Colvin studied discrimination. She thought things were unfair and wanted things to change. She studied African American history and joined the National Association for the Advancement of Colored People (NAACP). The NAACP fought to make laws fair.

SEPARATE RULES

Discrimination made Colvin angry. She wrote about it in school. She once shared this story about discrimination. For Easter, her mom said she could get a new pair of shoes, but black people couldn't try on shoes in stores. They had to trace their foot on paper at home. Then, they took the drawing to the store. They found shoes that matched it. Then, they took their shoes home. They had to hope the shoes would fit. Things like this made Colvin angry. White people had things easier than black people. She wanted to change this.

During the time of segregation, there were separate waiting rooms for black people and white people at bus stations.

Many people thought they couldn't change things. They thought white people would always be treated better. Colvin didn't agree. She was young, but that didn't matter. She could still be brave. She could create change.

Some people spoke out against segregation in the South.

CHAPTER 2

SITTING UP STRAIGHT

olvin made history on a day like any other. It was March 2, 1955. Schoolbooks lay on her lap. She sat near the window on a segregated bus. She had learned about segregation laws in school. They were called Jim Crow laws. For example, black people couldn't eat lunch at restaurant counters white people could eat at. She didn't think this was right.

RIDING THE BUS IN THE SOUTH

Black people had to sit in the back of the bus.

Colvin rode a city bus to school. She also rode it home. Many people rode the bus. Black people and white people could ride the same bus, but they couldn't sit together. The front of the bus was for white people. The back was for black people. The black part often had a sign that said "Colored."

Sometimes the white section was full. White people could then sit in the black part. Black people had to give up their seats. If no other seats were open, they had to stand.

THE DAY THAT CHANGED EVERYTHING

That March day in 1955, Colvin rode the bus home. The bus filled up. The driver told Colvin to move. She needed to go to the back. Colvin wouldn't move. She thought about the **US Constitution**. It says that all people have rights. Colvin told the bus driver this. "I have a constitutional right!" she said. The bus driver called the police.

The white police made fun of Colvin. They called her names. They bullied her, but Colvin didn't respond. Instead, she thought about other black leaders and brave women. Her teachers had told her about these people, such as Harriet Tubman. She helped slaves escape to freedom in the 1800s.

Segregated waiting rooms were all over the South.

Sojourner Truth was another. She used to be a slave. Then, she fought to end slavery.

Tubman and Truth were brave. They stood up for what was right. They stood up for black people. Colvin knew she could do this too.

She refused to give up her bus seat. The police arrested her. She wouldn't leave the bus quietly. First, she argued. Then, the police put her in handcuffs. They dragged her off the bus. She was kicking and screaming. Her schoolbooks went flying.

Sojourner Truth inspired Claudette Colvin.

FAST FACT

Segregation allowed white people to feel like they deserved better things than black people.

The month before, Colvin had learned about Marian Anderson. Anderson was an opera singer. She wasn't allowed to sing at a theater in Washington, DC, because she was black. She sang at the Lincoln Memorial instead. Colvin thought about all this on the day she was arrested.

AFTER THE BUS

Colvin was put in jail. She was scared. She was afraid she was going to have to go pick cotton. This is what they did to young people who were arrested.

Colvin's jail cell had bare walls. It had a bed. It had an open toilet. Luckily, she wasn't in jail for long. The person in charge of her church came. He paid money to get her out of jail. He told her she had done a great job, and she went home. She was changing things!

The police said Colvin had committed, or done, several crimes. However, Colvin wouldn't say she was guilty. She said she was right. The court agreed to drop some charges, but she was found guilty of one crime. The court said she attacked the police.

FAST FACT

In 1950, a Kansas school told Linda Brown that she couldn't attend because she was black. Brown later became part of a court case called *Brown v. Board of Education*. It brought an end to segregation everywhere.

Linda Brown won her court case.

SEPARATE BUT NOT EQUAL

All her life, Colvin had used segregated bathrooms. Her family members had gone to segregated hospitals. She had been educated in segregated schools. It was illegal for white people and "colored" people to marry each other. To be "colored" often meant being anyone who wasn't white. This meant that some Asian people were considered colored. Native Americans were also often considered colored. Colvin grew up when places were meant to be separate but equal. However, the places for "colored" people weren't as good as places for white people. These places weren't equal. They were worse. It was not equal at all.

Shown here is Claudette Colvin in 2005.

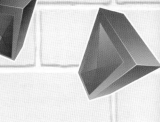

CHAPTER 3

A MORE EQUAL SOCIETY

Colvin was the first person to stay in her seat on the bus, but she was not the last. Rosa Parks did too. She refused to move from her seat on December 1, 1955. More women did this after Colvin and Parks.

REMEMBERING ROSA PARKS

Many people remember Rosa Parks. She is very famous today. People know she was brave, but Colvin was brave too. She was as important as Parks.

Rosa Parks (*right*) was the face of bus desegregation.

They both made others want to fight for their rights. More people stayed in their seats after that. More people cared about making everyone equal. A change began. But why do people remember Parks and not Colvin?

THE FACE OF THE PROTEST

The NAACP wanted an adult to be the face of a bus **protest** known as a boycott. Colvin was too young. She was a teenager. The NAACP chose Rosa Parks. She was an adult. Colvin understood their differences. She knew people would like Parks. Also,

Colvin's mother was happy they chose Parks. She didn't want her daughter to get in more trouble.

A LAWSUIT

In 1956, the NAACP filed a **lawsuit**. A lawsuit is a court case. This court case was called *Browder v. Gayle*. Colvin joined the lawsuit. They argued against bus segregation. They wanted people to be equal.

The state thought the laws were fair. They wanted to keep people separate. The court didn't agree. The court said that black people could sit in any seat.

FAST FACT

In 1960, a six-year-old girl named Ruby Bridges became the first African American to go to an all-white school in Louisiana.

ROSA PARKS AND CLAUDETTE COLVIN

Colvin and Parks knew each other. They met through church. Parks ran a youth group. She liked Colvin's story. She thought the group would like it. She asked Colvin to come speak. Colvin went there and told her story. She liked the group. She began to help with it. The group talked about unfair things. They wanted people to be equal.

CHANGE FOR ALL

Colvin was part of an important change. She helped change life for all black people in Alabama. She was part of the **civil rights movement**. The change in bus laws made other changes happen. Black people began to be treated better. Things slowly became more equal.

Ruby Bridges played a part in ending segregation too.

Rita Dove is a famous poet. She wrote a poem about Colvin. It's called "Claudette Colvin Goes to Work."

LIFE AFTER THE LAWSUIT

After the case, Colvin lost friends. She started going to college, but she had to drop out. Instead, she became a nurse's aide, or helper.

Colvin left Alabama in 1958. She went to New York. She lived with her older sister at first. Then, she got her own home. She worked in a nursing home. That's a place where old or sick people live. She worked there until 2004. Then, she retired.

CLAUDETTE COLVIN NOW

Colvin had two sons. One died in 1993. The other one lives in Georgia as of 2019. Colvin still lives in New York. She lives quietly. She doesn't talk about her brave past much. Many people remember Rosa Parks. Few remember Colvin. However, there are people who know she was important. In 2009, an

Claudette Colvin is shown here in 2009.

author wrote a book about her life. Many people are reading it now. Claudette Colvin is a woman to celebrate and remember.

TIMELINE

1939 Colvin is born. She is adopted by Q. P. and Mary Anne Colvin.

1955 On March 2, Colvin rides the bus home from school. She refuses to give up her seat for a white person. She is arrested.

1955 On December 1, Rosa Parks refuses to give up her seat on the bus. People around the United States hear about it.

1956 Colvin is part of a lawsuit. The court's decision ends bus segregation in Alabama.

1958 Colvin leaves Alabama for New York, where she still lives today.

2017 March 2 is officially declared Claudette Colvin Day in Montgomery, Alabama. This is to celebrate her brave actions on March 2, 1955.

GLOSSARY

activists People who work to change rules or laws.

civil rights movement A time in the 1950s and 1960s when people fought for equality.

discrimination Unfair treatment of a group of people.

lawsuit A legal dispute between two or more people or groups.

protest The act of showing a person doesn't like something or believes something is wrong.

segregation The act of setting someone or something apart from someone or something else.

US Constitution A document that gives rights to Americans and set up how the country is run.

FIND OUT MORE

BOOKS

Clinton, Chelsea. *She Persisted: 13 American Women Who Changed the World.* New York, NY: Philomel Books, 2017.

Hooks, Gwendolyn. *If You Were a Kid During the Civil Rights Movement.* New York, NY: Children's Press, 2017.

WEBSITE

Civil Rights Movements

http://www.historyforkids.net/civil-rights.html

VIDEO

The Girl Before Rosa Parks: Claudette Colvin

https://www.youtube.com/watch?v=qldCmA4ORoA

INDEX

Page numbers in **boldface** refer to images. Entries in **boldface** are glossary terms.

activists, 8
Anderson, Marian, 17
Bridges, Ruby, 23, **25**
Browder v. Gayle, 23
Brown v. Board of Education, 18
bus protest, 5–6, 13–18, 21
civil rights movement, 25
discrimination, 7–10, 17
Dove, Rita, 25

jail, 17–18
later life, **20**, 26–27, **27**
lawsuit, 23
NAACP, 8–9, 22–23
Parks, Rosa, 21–24, **22**, 26
Plessy v. Ferguson, 6
protest, **12**, 22
school, 8–10, 13, 15–17, 26
segregation, 5–7, 10, 13–14, **14**, 16, 18–19, 23
Truth, Sojourner, 16, **16**
Tubman, Harriet, 16
US Constitution, 15
Washington, Booker T., 8, **9**

ABOUT THE AUTHOR

Cathleen Small is a writer and editor. She has written more than sixty books for children and teens, on topics such as important people in history, war history, technology, and politics. When she's not writing, Small enjoys traveling with her family and spending time with her two young sons and their various pets. She lives in the San Francisco Bay Area.